20 best
chocolate
cupcake recipes

Houghton Mifflin Harcourt
Boston • New York • 2013

Copyright © 2013 by General Mills, Minneapolis, Minnesota. All rights reserved.

For information about permission to reproduce selections from this book, write to Permissions, Houghton Mifflin Harcourt Publishing Company, 215 Park Avenue South, New York, New York 10003.

www.hmhco.com

Cover photo: Aztec Chile-Chocolate Cupcakes (page 9)

General Mills
Food Content and Relationship Marketing Director: Geoff Johnson
Food Content Marketing Manager: Susan Klobuchar
Senior Editor: Grace Wells
Kitchen Manager: Ann Stuart
Recipe Development and Testing: Betty Crocker Kitchens
Photography: General Mills Photography Studios and Image Library

Houghton Mifflin Harcourt
Publisher: Natalie Chapman
Editorial Director: Cindy Kitchel
Executive Editor: Anne Ficklen
Associate Editor: Heather Dabah
Managing Editor: Rebecca Springer
Production Editor: Kristi Hart
Cover Design: Chrissy Kurpeski
Book Design: Tai Blanche

ISBN 978-0-544-31473-3
Printed in the United States of America

The Betty Crocker Kitchens seal guarantees success in your kitchen. Every recipe has been tested in America's Most Trusted Kitchens™ to meet our high standards of reliability, easy preparation and great taste.

FIND MORE GREAT IDEAS AT
Betty Crocker.com

Dear Friends,

This new collection of colorful mini books has been put together with you in mind because we know that you love great recipes and enjoy cooking and baking but have a busy lifestyle. So every little book in the series contains just 20 recipes for you to treasure and enjoy. Plus, each book is a single subject designed in a bite-size format just for you—it's easy to use and is filled with favorite recipes from the Betty Crocker Kitchens!

All of the books are conveniently divided into short chapters so you can quickly find what you're looking for, and the beautiful photos throughout are sure to entice you into making the delicious recipes. In the series, you'll discover a fabulous array of recipes to spark your interest—from cookies, cupcakes and birthday cakes to party ideas for a variety of occasions. There's grilled foods, potluck favorites and even gluten-free recipes too.

You'll love the variety in these mini books—so pick one or choose them all for your cooking pleasure.

Enjoy and happy cooking!

Sincerely,

Betty Crocker

contents

Simply Delicious
Chocolate Cupcakes • 6
Chocolate–Peanut Butter Cupcakes • 7
Sour Cream–Chocolate Cupcakes • 8
Aztec Chile-Chocolate Cupcakes • 9
Chocolate-Orange Cupcakes • 10
Chocolate-Espresso Cupcakes • 11
Mocha-Caramel Cappuccino Cupcakes • 12

Extra Chocolaty
Triple-Chocolate Mini Cups • 13
Chocolate Ganache Mini Cakes • 14
Truffle Lover's Cupcakes • 15
Chocolate-Hazelnut Cupcakes • 16
Frosted Chocolate Malt Cupcakes • 17
Double Dark Chocolate–Coconut Cupcakes • 18
Dark Chocolate Cupcakes • 19

Decadently Filled
Chocolate Chip–Cheesecake Swirl Cupcakes • 20
Mini Raspberry-Filled Chocolate Cupcakes • 21
Pecan Pie–Filled Chocolate Cupcakes • 22
Chocolate Whoopie Pie Cupcakes • 23
Banana-Turtle Torte Cupcakes • 24
Chocolate-Cherry Cupcakes • 25

Metric Conversion Guide • 26
Recipe Testing and Calculating Nutrition
  Information • 27

Simply Delicious

Chocolate Cupcakes

Prep Time: 20 Minutes • **Start to Finish:** 1 Hour 15 Minutes • Makes 24 cupcakes

2 cups Gold Medal® all-purpose flour
1¼ teaspoons baking soda
1 teaspoon salt
¼ teaspoon baking powder
1 cup hot water
⅔ cup unsweetened baking cocoa
¾ cup shortening
1½ cups sugar
2 eggs
1 teaspoon vanilla

1 Heat oven to 350°F. Place paper baking cup in each of 24 regular-size muffin cups.

2 In medium bowl, mix flour, baking soda, salt and baking powder; set aside. In small bowl, mix hot water and cocoa until dissolved; set aside.

3 In large bowl, beat shortening with electric mixer on medium speed 30 seconds. Gradually add sugar, about ¼ cup at a time, beating well after each addition and scraping bowl occasionally. Beat 2 minutes longer. Add eggs, one at a time, beating well after each addition. Beat in vanilla. On low speed, alternately add flour mixture, about one-third at a time, and cocoa mixture, about half at a time, beating just until blended.

4 Divide batter evenly among muffin cups, filling each with about 3 tablespoons batter or until about two-thirds full.

5 Bake 20 to 25 minutes or until toothpick inserted in center comes out clean. Cool 5 minutes. Remove cupcakes from pans; place on cooling racks. Cool completely, about 30 minutes. Frost with desired frosting.

1 Cupcake: Calories 160; Total Fat 7g (Saturated Fat 2g, Trans Fat 1g); Cholesterol 20mg; Sodium 180mg; Total Carbohydrate 22g (Dietary Fiber 1g); Protein 2g **Exchanges:** ½ Starch, 1 Other Carbohydrate, 1½ Fat **Carbohydrate Choices:** 1½

Mini Chocolate Cupcakes:
Place mini paper baking cup in each of 24 mini muffin cups. Make batter as directed in recipe. Fill each cup with about 1 tablespoon plus 1 teaspoon batter or until about two-thirds full. (Cover and refrigerate remaining batter until ready to bake; cool pan 15 minutes before reusing.) Bake 12 to 16 minutes or until toothpick inserted in center comes out clean. Cool 5 minutes. Remove cupcakes from pans; place on cooling racks. Cool completely, about 15 minutes. Repeat with remaining batter to make an additional 48 mini cupcakes. Frost with desired frosting. Makes 72 mini cupcakes.

Tip Did you know that baking cocoa can be stored for up to 2 years if kept in a cool, dark place?

Chocolate–Peanut Butter Cupcakes

Prep Time: 20 Minutes • **Start to Finish:** 1 Hour 10 Minutes • Makes 12 cupcakes

¾ cup granulated sugar

3 tablespoons creamy peanut butter

¼ cup fat-free sour cream

1 whole egg

1 egg white

1 cup Gold Medal all-purpose flour

¼ cup unsweetened baking cocoa

½ cup hot water

½ teaspoon baking soda

¼ cup miniature semisweet chocolate chips

Powdered sugar, if desired

1 Heat oven to 350°F. Place paper baking cup in each of 12 regular-size muffin cups.

2 In large bowl, beat granulated sugar, peanut butter, sour cream, egg and egg white with electric mixer on medium speed until well blended. Beat in remaining ingredients except powdered sugar on low speed just until mixed. Divide batter evenly among muffin cups.

3 Bake 15 to 20 minutes or until toothpick inserted in center comes out clean. Remove cupcakes from pan; place on cooling rack. Cool completely, about 30 minutes. Sprinkle tops with powdered sugar.

1 Cupcake: Calories 150; Total Fat 4g (Saturated Fat 1.5g, Trans Fat 0g); Cholesterol 20mg; Sodium 90mg; Total Carbohydrate 25g (Dietary Fiber 1g); Protein 4g **Exchanges:** ½ Starch, 1 Other Carbohydrate, 1 Fat **Carbohydrate Choices:** 1½

Tip Make your cupcakes stand out at the next bake sale or party. Sprinkle the top with powdered sugar just before wrapping or serving.

Sour Cream–Chocolate Cupcakes

Prep Time: 30 Minutes • **Start to Finish:** 1 Hour 25 Minutes • Makes 36 cupcakes

Cupcakes

- 2 cups Gold Medal all-purpose flour
- 2 cups granulated sugar
- 1¼ teaspoons baking soda
- 1 teaspoon salt
- ½ teaspoon baking powder
- 1 cup water
- ¾ cup sour cream
- ¼ cup shortening
- 1 teaspoon vanilla
- 2 eggs
- 4 oz unsweetened baking chocolate, melted, cooled

Rich Chocolate Buttercream Frosting

- 4 cups (1 lb) powdered sugar
- 1 cup butter or margarine, softened
- 3 tablespoons milk
- 1½ teaspoons vanilla
- 3 oz unsweetened baking chocolate, melted, cooled

1 Heat oven to 350°F. Place paper baking cup in each of 36 regular-size muffin cups.

2 In large bowl, beat all cupcake ingredients with electric mixer on low speed 30 seconds, scraping bowl constantly. Beat on high speed 3 minutes, scraping bowl occasionally. Divide batter evenly among muffin cups, filling each half full.

3 Bake 20 to 25 minutes or until toothpick inserted in center comes out clean. Remove cupcakes from pans; place on cooling racks. Cool completely, about 30 minutes.

4 In medium bowl, beat all frosting ingredients with electric mixer on medium speed until smooth and spreadable. If necessary, stir in additional milk, 1 teaspoon at a time. Spread frosting over cupcakes.

1 Cupcake: Calories 230; Total Fat 11g (Saturated Fat 6g, Trans Fat 0g); Cholesterol 30mg; Sodium 160mg; Total Carbohydrate 32g (Dietary Fiber 1g); Protein 2g **Exchanges:** ½ Starch, 1½ Other Carbohydrate, 2 Fat **Carbohydrate Choices:** 2

Variation:
To make cupcakes with a cake mix, place paper baking cup in each of 24 regular-size muffin cups. Make and bake 1 box Betty Crocker® SuperMoist® devil's food cake mix as directed on box, using ½ cup sour cream, ½ cup water, ⅓ cup vegetable oil and 2 eggs. Cool as directed. For the frosting, substitute 1 container (1 lb) Betty Crocker Rich & Creamy chocolate frosting. Makes 24 cupcakes.

Tip
Use ready-to-spread chocolate frosting instead of the homemade buttercream. You'll still get rave reviews for these sensational sweets!

Aztec Chile-Chocolate Cupcakes

Prep Time: 40 Minutes • **Start to Finish:** 2 Hours 20 Minutes • Makes 24 cupcakes

Cupcakes

- 2 cups Gold Medal all-purpose flour
- 3 teaspoons ancho chile pepper powder
- 1¼ teaspoons baking soda
- 1 teaspoon salt
- ¼ teaspoon baking powder
- ⅛ teaspoon ground red pepper (cayenne)
- 1 cup hot water
- ⅔ cup unsweetened baking cocoa
- ¾ cup shortening
- 1½ cups granulated sugar
- 2 eggs
- 1 teaspoon vanilla

Chocolate Shards

- 1 bag (11.5 oz) milk chocolate chips (2 cups)

Cinnamon-Chocolate Frosting

- ½ cup butter or margarine, softened
- 3 oz unsweetened baking chocolate, melted, cooled
- 3 cups powdered sugar
- ½ teaspoon ground cinnamon
- 1 tablespoon instant espresso coffee powder or granules
- About 3 tablespoons milk
- 2 teaspoons vanilla

1 Heat oven to 350°F. Place paper baking cup in each of 24 regular-size muffin cups.

2 In medium bowl, mix flour, chile pepper powder, baking soda, salt, baking powder and red pepper; set aside. In small bowl, mix hot water and cocoa until dissolved; set aside.

3 In large bowl, beat shortening with electric mixer on medium speed 30 seconds. Gradually add granulated sugar, about ¼ cup at a time, beating well after each addition and scraping bowl occasionally. Beat 2 minutes longer. Add eggs, one at a time, beating well after each addition. Beat in 1 teaspoon vanilla. On low speed, alternately add flour mixture, about one-third at a time, and cocoa mixture, about half at a time, beating just until blended.

4 Divide batter evenly among muffin cups, filling each with about 3 tablespoons or until about two-thirds full.

5 Bake 20 to 25 minutes or until toothpick inserted in center comes out clean. Cool 5 minutes. Remove cupcakes from pans; place on cooling racks. Cool completely, about 30 minutes.

6 Meanwhile, line cookie sheet with foil. In 1-quart saucepan, melt chocolate chips over low heat, stirring constantly, until smooth. Remove from heat. Spread chocolate to ⅛-inch thickness on cookie sheet. Refrigerate about 30 minutes or until set. Break into pieces; reserve.

7 In large bowl, mix butter and melted unsweetened chocolate. Stir in powdered sugar and cinnamon. Stir coffee powder into 2 tablespoons milk until dissolved. With spoon, beat coffee mixture into powdered sugar mixture. Stir in 2 teaspoons vanilla. Beat in additional milk, 1 teaspoon at a time, until smooth and spreadable. Frost cupcakes. Garnish with chocolate shards.

1 Cupcake: Calories 360; Total Fat 17g (Saturated Fat 8g, Trans Fat 1.5g); Cholesterol 30mg; Sodium 220mg; Total Carbohydrate 46g (Dietary Fiber 2g); Protein 3g **Exchanges:** 1 Starch, 2 Other Carbohydrate, 3½ Fat **Carbohydrate Choices:** 3

Tip To complete the Mexican-inspired theme, serve with dulce de leche ice cream.

Chocolate-Orange Cupcakes

Prep Time: 50 Minutes • **Start to Finish:** 1 Hour 50 Minutes • Makes 24 cupcakes

Cupcakes

2 cups Gold Medal all-purpose flour

1¼ teaspoons baking soda

1 teaspoon salt

¼ teaspoon baking powder

1 cup hot water

⅔ cup unsweetened baking cocoa

¾ cup shortening

1½ cups granulated sugar

2 eggs

1 teaspoon vanilla

2 tablespoons grated orange peel

Chocolate-Orange Frosting

½ cup butter or margarine, softened

3 oz unsweetened baking chocolate, melted, cooled

3 cups powdered sugar

2 teaspoons vanilla

2 to 3 tablespoons orange juice

Garnish

6 orange slice candies (wedges)

1 Heat oven to 350°F. Place paper baking cup in each of 24 regular-size muffin cups.

2 In medium bowl, mix flour, baking soda, salt and baking powder; set aside. In small bowl, mix hot water and cocoa until dissolved; set aside.

3 In large bowl, beat shortening with electric mixer on medium speed 30 seconds. Gradually add granulated sugar, about ¼ cup at a time, beating well after each addition and scraping bowl occasionally. Beat 2 minutes longer. Add eggs, one at a time, beating well after each addition. Beat in 1 teaspoon vanilla and orange peel. On low speed, alternately add flour mixture, about one-third at a time, and cocoa mixture, about half at a time, beating just until blended.

4 Divide batter evenly among muffin cups, filling each with about 3 tablespoons or until about two-thirds full.

5 Bake 20 to 25 minutes or until toothpick inserted in center comes out clean. Cool 5 minutes. Remove cupcakes from pans; place on cooling racks. Cool completely, about 30 minutes.

6 In large bowl, mix butter and melted chocolate until blended. Stir in powdered sugar. Beat in 2 teaspoons vanilla and 2 tablespoons orange juice until smooth. If necessary, beat in additional orange juice, 1 teaspoon at a time, until frosting is spreadable. Frost cupcakes.

7 Cut each orange slice candy horizontally in half; cut each half equally into 6 pieces. Garnish each cupcake with 3 pieces of candy.

1 Cupcake: Calories 300; Total Fat 13g (Saturated Fat 6g, Trans Fat 1g); Cholesterol 30mg; Sodium 210mg; Total Carbohydrate 43g (Dietary Fiber 2g); Protein 2g **Exchanges:** 1 Starch, 2 Other Carbohydrate, 2½ Fat **Carbohydrate Choices:** 3

Tip If you don't have orange slices, use orange sprinkles instead — they'll be just as pretty!

Chocolate-Espresso Cupcakes

Prep Time: 15 Minutes • **Start to Finish:** 1 Hour 15 Minutes • Makes 12 cupcakes

1 cup Gold Medal all-purpose flour
½ cup unsweetened baking cocoa
½ teaspoon baking soda
¼ teaspoon salt
2 egg whites
1 whole egg
1 cup granulated sugar
¼ cup canola or vegetable oil
½ cup light chocolate soymilk
2 teaspoons instant espresso coffee granules
1½ teaspoons vanilla
Powdered sugar, if desired

1 Heat oven to 375°F. Lightly spray 12 regular-size muffin cups with cooking spray, or line with paper baking cups.

2 In medium bowl, mix flour, cocoa, baking soda and salt. In another medium bowl, beat egg whites, whole egg, granulated sugar and oil with electric mixer on medium-high speed 1 to 2 minutes or until well mixed. On low speed, alternately add flour mixture and soymilk, beating after each addition, until well blended. Add coffee granules and vanilla; beat on low speed 30 seconds. Divide batter evenly among muffin cups, filling each with about 3 tablespoons batter.

3 Bake 15 to 20 minutes or until toothpick inserted in center of cupcake comes out clean. Cool 10 minutes. Remove cupcakes from pan; place on cooling rack. Cook completely, about 30 minutes.

4 Just before serving, sift powdered sugar over tops of cupcakes.

1 Cupcake: Calories 170; Total Fat 6g (Saturated Fat 1g, Trans Fat 0g); Cholesterol 20mg; Sodium 125mg; Total Carbohydrate 27g (Dietary Fiber 1g); Protein 3g **Exchanges:** ½ Starch, 1½ Other Carbohydrate, 1 Fat **Carbohydrate Choices:** 2

Raspberry-Chocolate Cupcakes:
Omit the vanilla and the espresso powder. Add 2 teaspoons raspberry extract with the soymilk. Serve with fresh raspberries.

Simply Delicious

Mocha-Caramel Cappuccino Cupcakes

Prep Time: 20 Minutes • **Start to Finish:** 1 Hour 20 Minutes • Makes 6 jumbo cupcakes

Cupcakes

- 2 cups Gold Medal all-purpose flour
- 1¼ teaspoons baking soda
- 1 teaspoon salt
- ¼ teaspoon baking powder
- 1 cup hot water
- ⅔ cup unsweetened baking cocoa
- 4 teaspoons instant espresso coffee powder or granules
- ¾ cup shortening
- 1½ cups granulated sugar
- 2 eggs
- 1 teaspoon vanilla

Topping

- 1 cup whipping cream
- 2 tablespoons powdered sugar
- ¾ teaspoon instant espresso coffee powder or granules
- 2 tablespoons miniature semisweet chocolate chips
- 2 tablespoons caramel topping

1 Heat oven to 350°F. Place jumbo paper baking cup in each of 6 jumbo muffin cups, grease bottoms and sides of muffin cups with shortening and lightly flour, or spray with baking spray with flour.

2 In medium bowl, mix flour, baking soda, salt and baking powder; set aside. In small bowl, mix hot water, cocoa and 4 teaspoons coffee powder until dissolved; set aside.

3 In large bowl, beat shortening with electric mixer on medium speed 30 seconds. Gradually add granulated sugar, about ¼ cup at a time, beating well after each addition and scraping bowl occasionally. Beat 2 minutes longer. Add eggs, one at a time, beating well after each addition. Beat in vanilla. On low speed, alternately add flour mixture, about one-third at a time, and cocoa mixture, about half at a time, beating just until blended.

4 Divide batter evenly among muffin cups, filling each with about ½ cup batter or until about two-thirds full.

5 Bake 20 to 25 minutes or until toothpick inserted in center comes out clean. Cool 5 minutes. Remove cupcakes from pan; place on cooling rack. Cool completely, about 30 minutes.

6 In small deep bowl, beat whipping cream, powdered sugar and ¾ teaspoon coffee powder with electric mixer on high speed until stiff peaks form.

7 To serve, place each cupcake in a coffee cup, if desired. Top each with about 3 tablespoons whipped cream; sprinkle with 1 teaspoon chocolate chips and drizzle with 1 teaspoon caramel topping.

1 Cupcake: Calories 840; Total Fat 45g (Saturated Fat 18g, Trans Fat 5g); Cholesterol 125mg; Sodium 740mg; Total Carbohydrate 99g (Dietary Fiber 5g); Protein 9g **Exchanges:** 3½ Starch, 3 Other Carbohydrate, 8½ Fat **Carbohydrate Choices:** 6½

Tip For a quick and easy topping, use whipped topping from an aerosol can.

Extra Chocolaty

Triple-Chocolate Mini Cups

Prep Time: 35 Minutes • **Start to Finish:** 2 Hours 25 Minutes • Makes 72 mini cups

- ¾ cup butter or margarine
- 4 oz unsweetened baking chocolate
- 2 cups sugar
- 1½ cups Gold Medal all-purpose flour
- ½ cup unsweetened baking cocoa
- 2 teaspoons baking powder
- ½ teaspoon salt
- 4 eggs
- 1½ cups semisweet chocolate chips
- 6 dozen whole candied cherries, Hershey®'s Kisses® Brand milk chocolates*, unwrapped or pecan halves

1 Heat oven to 350°F. Place mini paper baking cups in each of 72 mini muffin cups OR use mini foil muffin cups if you don't have mini muffin pans.

2 In 2-quart saucepan, melt butter and chocolate over low heat 6 to 10 minutes, stirring occasionally, until smooth. Cool 20 minutes. In large bowl, beat melted chocolate mixture, sugar, 1 cup of the flour, the cocoa, baking powder, salt and eggs with electric mixer on medium speed about 2 minutes, scraping bowl occasionally, until well blended. Stir in remaining ½ cup flour and the chocolate chips. Drop dough by rounded teaspoons into mini cups.

3 Bake 15 to 17 minutes or until edges are slightly firm (center will be slightly soft). Immediately top each with cherry, milk chocolate candy or pecan half and pressing slightly. Cool completely, about 1 hour.

The HERSHEY'S® KISSES® trademark and trade dress and the Conical figure and plume device are used under license.

1 Mini Cup: Calories 100; Total Fat 4g (Saturated Fat 2.5g, Trans Fat 0g); Cholesterol 15mg; Sodium 55mg; Total Carbohydrate 15g (Dietary Fiber 0g); Protein 1g **Exchanges:** 1 Other Carbohydrate, 1 Fat **Carbohydrate Choices:** 1

Extra Chocolaty • **13**

Chocolate Ganache Mini Cakes

Prep Time: 45 Minutes • **Start to Finish:** 1 Hour 55 Minutes • Makes 60 mini cakes

1 Heat oven to 350°F (325°F for dark or nonstick pans). Place miniature paper baking cup in each of 60 mini muffin cups. Make cake batter as directed on box. Divide batter evenly among muffin cups, filling each with about 1 heaping tablespoon batter or until three-fourths full.

2 Bake 10 to 15 minutes or until toothpick inserted in center comes out clean. Cool 5 minutes. Remove cupcakes from pans to cooling racks. Cool completely, about 30 minutes.

Mini Cakes
1 box Betty Crocker SuperMoist devil's food cake mix

Water, vegetable oil and eggs called for on cake mix box

Filling
⅔ cup raspberry jam

Ganache and Garnish
6 oz dark baking chocolate, chopped

⅔ cup whipping cream

1 tablespoon raspberry-flavored liqueur, if desired

Fresh raspberries, if desired

3 Place chocolate in medium bowl. In 1-quart saucepan, heat whipping cream just to boiling; pour over chocolate. Let stand 3 to 5 minutes until chocolate is melted and smooth when stirred. Stir in liqueur. Let stand 15 minutes, stirring occasionally, until mixture coats spoon.

4 Meanwhile, by slowly spinning end of round handle of wooden spoon back and forth, make deep, ½-inch-wide indentation in center of top of each cupcake, not quite to bottom (wiggle end of spoon in cupcake to make opening large enough).

5 Spoon jam into small resealable food-storage plastic bag; seal bag. Cut ⅜-inch tip off 1 bottom corner of bag. Insert tip of bag into opening in each cupcake; squeeze bag to fill opening.

6 Spoon about 1 teaspoon ganache onto each mini cake. Garnish each with raspberry. Store loosely covered.

1 Mini Cake: Calories 80; Total Fat 5g (Saturated Fat 2g, Trans Fat 0g); Cholesterol 15mg; Sodium 65mg; Total Carbohydrate 9g (Dietary Fiber 0g); Protein 1g **Exchanges:** ½ Starch, 1 Fat **Carbohydrate Choices:** ½

Tip If you refrigerate these mini cakes, let them stand at room temperature at least 20 minutes before serving.

Truffle Lover's Cupcakes

Prep Time: 35 Minutes • **Start to Finish:** 1 Hour 50 Minutes • Makes 24 cupcakes

Cupcakes

¾ cup miniature semisweet chocolate chips

1 box Betty Crocker SuperMoist chocolate fudge cake mix

1 cup water

½ cup vegetable oil

3 eggs

3 tablespoons hazelnut- or orange-flavored liqueur

Ganache

⅓ cup whipping cream

½ cup miniature semisweet chocolate chips

1 Heat oven to 350°F (325°F for dark or nonstick pans). Place paper baking cup in each of 24 regular-size muffin cups. In small bowl, toss chocolate chips with 1 tablespoon of the cake mix. In large bowl, beat remaining cake mix, the water, oil and eggs with electric mixer on low speed 30 seconds, then on medium speed 2 minutes, scraping bowl occasionally. Stir in coated chocolate chips. Divide batter evenly among muffin cups.

2 Bake as directed on box for 24 cupcakes. Cool 10 minutes. Remove from pans; place on cooling racks. Immediately prick holes in tops of cupcakes with toothpick. Brush about ½ teaspoon liqueur over each cupcake. Cool completely, about 30 minutes.

3 In heavy 1-quart saucepan, heat whipping cream over medium-high heat until hot but not boiling; remove from heat. Stir in ½ cup chocolate chips until melted. Let stand 10 minutes. Dip tops of cupcakes in ganache. Top with miniature chocolate chips, grated orange peel or ground hazelnuts, if desired. Store loosely covered.

1 Cupcake: Calories 180; Total Fat 10g (Saturated Fat 3.5g, Trans Fat 0g); Cholesterol 30mg; Sodium 170mg; Total Carbohydrate 20g (Dietary Fiber 1g); Protein 2g **Exchanges:** ½ Starch, 1 Other Carbohydrate, 2 Fat **Carbohydrate Choices:** 1

Tip If you have only one pan and a recipe calls for more cupcakes than your pan will make, cover and refrigerate the rest of the batter while baking the first batch. Cool the pan about 15 minutes, then bake the rest of the batter, adding 1 to 2 minutes to the bake time.

Chocolate-Hazelnut Cupcakes

Prep Time: 30 Minutes • **Start to Finish:** 1 Hour 20 Minutes • Makes 24 cupcakes

Cupcakes

- 1 cup Gold Medal self-rising flour
- ½ teaspoon salt
- ¼ cup unsalted butter or regular butter, softened
- ½ cup sugar
- 1 teaspoon vanilla
- ½ teaspoon almond extract
- 1½ cups hazelnut spread with cocoa (16 oz)
- 4 eggs
- ¼ cup milk

Ganache

- 6 oz bittersweet chocolate chips (1 cup)
- 3 tablespoons unsalted butter or regular butter
- 4 teaspoons light corn syrup
- ¼ teaspoon vanilla
- ⅓ to ½ cup chopped hazelnuts, toasted*

1 Heat oven to 325°F. Place paper baking cup in each of 24 regular-size muffin cups. In small bowl, stir flour and salt until mixed; set aside.

2 In large bowl, beat ¼ cup softened butter with electric mixer on medium speed until creamy. Add sugar, 1 teaspoon vanilla and the almond extract; beat until light and fluffy. Add hazelnut spread; beat until well blended, scraping bowl occasionally. Add eggs; beat until smooth. Add half of the flour mixture; beat on low speed just until blended. Add milk; beat until blended. Gently stir in remaining flour until batter is smooth. Divide batter evenly among muffin cups, filling each about half full.

3 Bake 20 to 25 minutes or until set. Cool completely in pan, about 30 minutes.

4 Meanwhile, in small microwavable bowl, microwave chocolate chips, 3 tablespoons butter and the corn syrup on High 1 to 1½ minutes, stirring every 30 seconds, until chips are melted and mixture is smooth. Stir in ¼ teaspoon vanilla. Top cooled cupcakes with ganache. Sprinkle with hazelnuts.

To toast hazelnuts, heat oven to 350°F. Spread hazelnuts in ungreased shallow pan. Bake uncovered 6 to 10 minutes, stirring occasionally, until light brown.

1 Cupcake: Calories 130; Total Fat 9g (Saturated Fat 4g, Trans Fat 0g); Cholesterol 45mg; Sodium 80mg; Total Carbohydrate 11g (Dietary Fiber 1g); Protein 2g **Exchanges:** ½ Starch, 2 Fat **Carbohydrate Choices:** 1

Tip Hazelnut spread with cocoa can be found near the peanut butter, jams and preserves in your grocery store.

Frosted Chocolate Malt Cupcakes

Prep Time: 30 Minutes • **Start to Finish:** 1 Hour 20 Minutes • Makes 16 cupcakes

Cupcakes

1½ cups Original Bisquick® mix

¾ cup granulated sugar

⅓ cup unsweetened baking cocoa

¼ cup chocolate-flavor malted milk powder

⅔ cup milk

¼ cup vegetable oil

1 teaspoon vanilla

2 eggs

Frosting

2 tablespoons chocolate-flavor malted milk powder

2 tablespoons milk

2 cups powdered sugar

1 tablespoon unsweetened baking cocoa

¼ cup butter or margarine, softened

1 Heat oven to 400°F. Place paper baking cup in each of 16 regular-size muffin cups. In large bowl, beat all cupcake ingredients with electric mixer on low speed 30 seconds, scraping bowl constantly. Beat on medium speed 4 minutes, scraping bowl occasionally. Divide batter evenly among muffin cups.

2 Bake 15 to 20 minutes or until toothpick inserted in center comes out clean. Immediately remove cupcakes from pans; place on cooling racks. Cool completely, about 30 minutes.

3 In medium bowl, stir 2 tablespoons malted milk powder and 2 tablespoons milk until blended; let stand 5 minutes. Add remaining frosting ingredients; beat with electric mixer on medium speed 1 to 2 minutes or until smooth. Frost cupcakes.

1 Cupcake: Calories 230; Total Fat 9g (Saturated Fat 3.5g, Trans Fat 0.5g); Cholesterol 35mg; Sodium 180mg; Total Carbohydrate 35g (Dietary iber 1g); Protein 3g **Exchanges:** 1 Starch, 1½ Other Carbohydrate, 1½ Fat **Carbohydrate Choices:** 2

Tip Double your malted milk pleasure by pressing coarsely chopped malted milk balls on top of the frosted cupcakes.

Extra Chocolaty

Double Dark Chocolate–Coconut Cupcakes

Prep Time: 40 Minutes • **Start to Finish:** 1 Hour 20 Minutes • Makes 12 cupcakes

A dark chocolate cupcake topped with chocolate-coconut frosting and a bonus mini cupcake. The real surprise? It's an egg-free, dairy-free vegan recipe.

1 Heat oven to 350°F. Place paper baking cup in each of 12 mini and 12 regular-size muffin cups. In large bowl, using whisk, mix flour, granulated sugar, ½ cup cocoa, the baking soda and salt. In medium bowl, using whisk, mix soymilk, canola oil, vinegar and 1½ teaspoons vanilla. Pour soymilk mixture into flour mixture; beat with whisk until well mixed. Stir in chocolate chips. Fill each mini muffin cup with 1 level measuring tablespoon batter. Divide remaining batter evenly among regular-size muffin cups.

2 Bake mini cupcakes 12 to 16 minutes or until toothpick inserted in center comes out clean. Bake regular-size cupcakes 22 to 26 minutes or until toothpick inserted in center comes out clean. Cool 10 minutes. Remove cupcakes from pans; place on cooling racks. Cool completely, about 30 minutes.

3 In large bowl, beat vegetable oil spread, coconut oil, 1 teaspoon vanilla and 2 teaspoons of the water with electric mixer on low speed until smooth. Beat in 3 tablespoons cocoa and the powdered sugar, 1 cup at a time. Gradually beat in just enough remaining water until smooth and spreadable.

4 To assemble cupcake stacks, remove paper baking cups. Pipe frosting on top of 1 regular-size cupcake. Top with 1 mini cupcake; frost top of mini cupcake. Repeat with remaining cupcakes and frosting. Garnish with chocolate curls and coconut, if desired.

Cupcakes

- 1½ cups Gold Medal all-purpose flour
- 1 cup granulated sugar
- ½ cup unsweetened baking cocoa
- 1 teaspoon baking soda
- ½ teaspoon salt
- 1 cup original- or vanilla-flavored soymilk
- ½ cup canola oil or vegetable oil
- 1 tablespoon cider vinegar
- 1½ teaspoons vanilla
- ½ cup miniature vegan chocolate chips

Chocolate-Coconut Frosting

- ½ cup vegan vegetable oil spread stick, softened
- ⅓ cup virgin unrefined coconut oil (solid, not melted)
- 1 teaspoon vanilla
- 2 to 4 teaspoons water
- 3 tablespoons unsweetened baking cocoa
- 3 cups sifted powdered sugar

1 Cupcake: Calories 490; Total Fat 24g (Saturated Fat 9g, Trans Fat 0g); Cholesterol 0mg; Sodium 280mg; Total Carbohydrate 66g (Dietary Fiber 2g); Protein 3g **Exchanges:** 1 Starch, 3½ Other Carbohydrate, 4½ Fat **Carbohydrate Choices:** 4½

Tip Always read labels to make sure each recipe ingredient is vegan. If you're unsure about any ingredient or product, check with the manufacturer.

Dark Chocolate Cupcakes

Prep Time: 45 Minutes • **Start to Finish:** 2 Hours • Makes 12 cupcakes

Chocolate Shards
2 tablespoons dark chocolate chips (1 oz)

Frosting
1⅓ cups dark chocolate chips
¼ cup butter, cut into small pieces
1 cup whipping cream

Cupcakes
1 cup Gold Medal all-purpose flour
¾ teaspoon baking soda
½ teaspoon salt
¼ teaspoon baking powder
½ cup boiling water
⅓ cup unsweetened baking cocoa
½ cup butter or margarine
¾ cup sugar
½ teaspoon vanilla
1 egg

1 In small microwavable bowl, microwave 2 tablespoons chocolate chips uncovered on High 1 minute, until melted, stirring once after 30 seconds. Pour chocolate onto 12 x 10-inch sheet of waxed paper; spread in thin layer, forming 3 x 3-inch square. Place second 12 x 10-inch sheet of waxed paper over chocolate square; press to release air bubbles. Roll waxed paper tightly into a cylinder. Refrigerate until set.

2 In medium bowl, place 1⅓ cups chocolate chips and ¼ cup butter. In small microwavable bowl, microwave whipping cream on High about 1 minute or until cream just begins to simmer. Pour cream over chips and butter; beat with whisk until chocolate is melted and mixture is smooth and shiny. Refrigerate 30 to 45 minutes or until completely cooled, stirring occasionally.

3 Heat oven to 350°F. Place paper baking cup in each of 12 regular-size muffin cups. In medium bowl, mix flour, baking soda, salt and baking powder; set aside. In small bowl, mix boiling water and cocoa until dissolved.

4 In large bowl, beat ½ cup butter with electric mixer on medium speed 30 seconds. Gradually add sugar, beating well. Beat 2 minutes longer. Beat in vanilla and egg until blended. On low speed, alternately add flour mixture and cocoa mixture, beating just until blended. Divide batter evenly among muffin cups. Bake 20 to 25 minutes or until toothpick inserted in center comes out clean. Cool 5 minutes. Remove cupcakes from pan; place on cooling racks. Cool completely.

5 In medium bowl, beat all frosting ingredients with electric mixer on medium speed until light and fluffy, about 30 seconds (Do not overbeat.) Fit decorating bag with large star tip. Fill bag with frosting. Pipe frosting in circular motion on top of each cupcake, mounding frosting slightly in center.

6 Unroll waxed-paper cylinder, causing chocolate to crack creating shards. Garnish each cupcake with chocolate shards. Store in refrigerator.

1 Cupcake: Calories 380; Total Fat 25g (Saturated Fat 16g, Trans Fat 0.5g); Cholesterol 70mg; Sodium 290mg; Total Carbohydrate 35g (Dietary Fiber 2g); Protein 3g **Exchanges:** 2½ Other Carbohydrate, 5 Fat **Carbohydrate Choices:** 2

Tip These cupcakes should be stored in the refrigerator. To serve, allow them to stand at room temperature for about 15 minutes before serving.

Decadently Filled

Chocolate Chip–Cheesecake Swirl Cupcakes

Prep Time: 30 Minutes • **Start to Finish:** 1 Hour 5 Minutes • Makes 24 cupcakes

½ cup sugar

2 packages (3 oz each) cream cheese, softened

1 egg

1 bag (6 oz) semisweet chocolate chips (1 cup)

2¼ cups Gold Medal all-purpose flour

1⅔ cups sugar

¼ cup unsweetened baking cocoa

1¼ cups water

½ cup vegetable oil

2 tablespoons white vinegar

2 teaspoons baking soda

2 teaspoons vanilla

1 teaspoon salt

1 Heat oven to 350°F. Place paper baking cup in each of 24 regular-size muffin cups. In medium bowl, beat ½ cup sugar and the cream cheese with electric mixer on medium speed until smooth. Beat in egg. Stir in chocolate chips; set aside.

2 In large bowl, beat remaining ingredients on low speed 30 seconds, scraping bowl occasionally. Beat on high speed 3 minutes, scraping bowl occasionally. Reserve 1½ cups batter.

3 Divide batter evenly among muffin cups, filling each with 1 rounded tablespoon batter or until about one-third full. Spoon 1 tablespoon cream cheese mixture onto batter in each cup. Top each with reserved batter (½ rounded tablespoon).

4 Bake 30 to 35 minutes or until toothpick inserted in center comes out clean. Store in refrigerator.

1 Cupcake: Calories 220; Total Fat 10g (Saturated Fat 3.5g; Trans Fat 0g); Cholesterol 15mg; Sodium 230mg; Total Carbohydrate 32g (Dietary Fiber 1g); Protein 2g **Exchanges:** ½ Starch, 1½ Other Carbohydrate, 2 Fat **Carbohydrate Choices:** 2

Tip These cupcakes with a cream cheese swirl are great for picnics. They can be made the day before, so you can have them ready to serve to kids of all ages!

Mini Raspberry-Filled Chocolate Cupcakes

Prep Time: 1 Hour • **Start to Finish:** 1 Hour 35 Minutes • Makes 60 mini cupcakes

1 box Betty Crocker SuperMoist devil's food cake mix

Water, vegetable oil and eggs called for on cake mix box

²⁄₃ cup seedless raspberry jam

1 cup fresh or frozen (thawed) raspberries

1 container (12 oz) Better Crocker Whipped fluffy white frosting

60 fresh raspberries (from three 6-oz containers)

1 Heat oven to 350°F (325°F for dark or nonstick pans). Place mini paper baking cup in each of 60 mini muffin cups.

2 Make cake mix as directed on box, using water, oil and eggs. Divide batter evenly among muffin cups, filling each with 1 rounded tablespoon batter or until about three-fourths full.

3 Bake 10 to 15 minutes or until toothpick inserted in center comes out clean. Cool 5 minutes. Remove cupcakes from pans; place on cooling racks. Cool completely, about 15 minutes.

4 By slowly spinning end of round handle of wooden spoon back and forth, make deep, ½-inch-wide indentation in center of top of each cupcake, not quite to bottom (wiggle end of spoon in mini cake to make opening large enough).

5 Spoon jam into small resealable food-storage plastic bag; seal bag. Cut ⅜-inch tip off 1 bottom corner of bag. Insert tip of bag into opening in each cupcake; squeeze bag to fill opening.

6 In blender, place 1 cup raspberries. Cover; pulse 20 seconds or until pureed. Press puree through small strainer to remove seeds. Pour ¼ cup raspberry puree into medium bowl; stir in frosting until well mixed. Frost cupcakes. Garnish each cupcake with 1 raspberry.

1 Mini Cupcake: Calories 80; Total Fat 3g (Saturated Fat 1g, Trans Fat 0g); Cholesterol 10mg; Sodium 85mg; Total Carbohydrate 13g (Dietary Fiber 0g); Protein 0g **Exchanges:** 1 Other Carbohydrate, ½ Fat **Carbohydrate Choices:** 1

Tip These little cupcakes would dazzle your guests served on a pedestal platter.

Pecan Pie–Filled Chocolate Cupcakes

Prep Time: 40 Minutes • **Start to Finish:** 2 Hours 10 Minutes • Makes 24 cupcakes

Cupcakes

1 box Betty Crocker SuperMoist devil's food or other flavor cake mix

Water, vegetable oil and eggs called for on cake mix box

Pecan Pie Filling

¼ cup granulated sugar

¼ cup packed brown sugar

2 tablespoons cornstarch

¾ cup light corn syrup

¼ cup butter melted

½ teaspoon salt

2 eggs, slightly beaten

1 cup chopped pecans, toasted*

1 teaspoon vanilla

Spiced-Cream Frosting

3 teaspoons unflavored gelatin

¼ cup cold water

3 cups heavy whipping cream

⅔ cup powdered sugar

1½ teaspoons vanilla

Garnish, if desired

½ teaspoon ground cinnamon

24 candied pecans

1 Heat oven to 350°F (325°F for dark or nonstick pans). Place paper baking cup in each of 24 regular-size muffin cups. Make and bake cake mix as directed on box for 24 cupcakes. Cool 10 minutes. Remove cupcakes from pans; place on cooling racks. Cool completely, about 30 minutes.

2 Meanwhile, in 2-quart saucepan, combine granulated sugar, brown sugar and cornstarch. Stir in corn syrup, melted butter, salt and eggs. Cook over medium heat, stirring constantly, just until mixture begins to boil; remove from heat. Stir in toasted pecans and 1 teaspoon vanilla. Let stand 10 minutes. Refrigerate 1 hour or until thickened.

3 In 1-quart saucepan, sprinkle gelatin over water to soften; let stand 1 minute. Heat over low heat about 2 minutes, stirring constantly, until gelatin is dissolved. Let stand about 15 minutes, stirring frequently, until cooled to room temperature.

4 In chilled large bowl, beat whipping cream with electric mixer on low speed, slowly adding cooled gelatin. Increase speed to medium; beat until soft peaks form. Add powdered sugar and 1½ teaspoons vanilla; beat until stiff peaks form. Refrigerate until ready to frost cupcakes.

5 With melon baller, scoop out center of each cupcake almost to bottom of cupcake; spoon 1 tablespoon filling into cavity of each. In 1-quart resealable food-storage plastic bag, cut ¼-inch opening diagonally across bottom corner of bag; fit ½-inch star tip in opening. Spoon spiced-cream frosting into bag; seal bag. Pipe frosting onto cupcakes in circular motion. Refrigerate cupcakes until ready to serve.

6 Just before serving, sprinkle cinnamon over cupcakes and garnish each cupcake with candied pecan. Store cupcakes loosely covered in refrigerator.

To toast pecans, heat oven to 350°F. Spread pecans in ungreased shallow pan. Bake uncovered 6 to 10 minutes, stirring occasionally, until light brown.

1 Cupcake: Calories 420; Total Fat 26g (Saturated Fat 12g, Trans Fat 0.5g); Cholesterol 95mg; Sodium 270mg; Total Carbohydrate 40g (Dietary Fiber 1g); Protein 5g **Exchanges:** 1½ Starch, 1 Other Carbohydrate, 5 Fat **Carbohydrate Choices:** 2½

Tip To make candied pecans, melt 1½ teaspoons butter in 7-inch skillet over low heat. Stir in 1½ teaspoons sugar. Add pecans; turn pecans several times to coat with sugar mixture. Candied pecans can also be purchased at the grocery store; look for them in the bulk section or with the snack nuts.

Chocolate Whoopie Pie Cupcakes

Prep Time: 30 Minutes • **Start to Finish:** 1 Hour 25 Minutes • Makes 24 cupcakes

Cupcakes

2 cups Gold Medal all-purpose flour
1¼ teaspoons baking soda
1 teaspoon salt
¼ teaspoon baking powder
1 cup hot water
⅔ cup unsweetened baking cocoa
¾ cup shortening
1½ cups sugar
2 eggs
1 teaspoon vanilla

Filling

1 cup Betty Crocker Whipped fluffy white frosting (from 12-oz container)
¾ cup marshmallow creme

1 Heat oven to 350°F. Place paper baking cup in each of 24 regular-size muffin cups.

2 In medium bowl, mix flour, baking soda, salt and baking powder; set aside. In small bowl, mix hot water and cocoa until dissolved; set aside.

3 In large bowl, beat shortening with electric mixer on medium speed 30 seconds. Gradually add sugar, about ¼ cup at a time, beating well after each addition and scraping bowl occasionally. Beat 2 minutes longer. Add eggs, one at a time, beating well after each addition. Beat in vanilla. On low speed, alternately add flour mixture, about one-third at a time, and cocoa mixture, about half at a time, beating just until blended.

4 Divide batter evenly among muffin cups, filling each with about 3 tablespoons batter or until about two-thirds full.

5 Bake 20 to 25 minutes or until toothpick inserted in center comes out clean. Cool 5 minutes. Remove cupcakes from pans; place on cooling racks. Cool completely, about 30 minutes.

6 In small bowl, mix frosting and marshmallow creme. Cut cupcakes crosswise into halves. Spread about 1 tablespoon filling on each cupcake bottom; replace cupcake tops.

1 Cupcake: Calories 210; Total Fat 9g (Saturated Fat 2.5g, Trans Fat 1.5g); Cholesterol 20mg; Sodium 190mg; Total Carbohydrate 29g (Dietary Fiber 1g); Protein 2g **Exchanges:** 1 Starch, 1 Other Carbohydrate, 1½ Fat **Carbohydrate Choices:** 2

Tip Save time by using 1 box Betty Crocker Super-Moist devil's food cake mix instead of making cupcakes from scratch. Make and bake cake mix as directed on box for cupcakes. Cool and fill as directed in recipe.

Banana-Turtle Torte Cupcakes

Prep Time: 55 Minutes • **Start to Finish:** 2 Hours • Makes 24 cupcakes

Cupcakes

2 cups Gold Medal all-purpose flour
1¼ teaspoons baking soda
1 teaspoon salt
¼ teaspoon baking powder
1 cup hot water
⅔ cup unsweetened baking cocoa
¾ cup shortening
1½ cups granulated sugar
2 eggs
1 teaspoon vanilla
¾ cup chopped pecans
1 pint (2 cups) whipping cream
2 medium bananas

Caramel Sauce

¼ cup butter
½ cup packed brown sugar
2 tablespoons corn syrup
1 tablespoon milk
24 whole pecans

1 Heat oven to 350°F. Place paper baking cup in each of 24 regular-size muffin cups. In medium bowl, mix flour, baking soda, salt and baking powder; set aside. In small bowl, mix hot water and cocoa until dissolved; set aside.

2 In large bowl, beat shortening with electric mixer on medium speed 30 seconds. Gradually add granulated sugar, about ¼ cup at a time, beating well after each addition and scraping bowl occasionally. Beat 2 minutes longer. Add eggs, one at a time, beating well after each addition. Beat in vanilla. On low speed, alternately add flour mixture, about one-third of mixture at a time and cocoa mixture, about half at a time, beating just until blended. Stir in pecans. Divide batter evenly among muffin cups, filling each about two-thirds full.

3 In chilled large bowl, beat whipping cream with electric mixer on high speed until stiff peaks form. Cut cupcakes crosswise into halves.

4 In 1-quart saucepan, melt butter over medium-high heat. Stir in brown sugar, corn syrup and milk. Cool 5 minutes.

5 Spread 1 heaping tablespoon whipped cream on each cupcake bottom. Thinly slice bananas; place 3 slices on top of whipped cream on each cupcake. Drizzle with 1 teaspoon caramel sauce; replace cupcake tops. Spread remaining whipped cream on cupcakes; drizzle with 1 teaspoon caramel sauce. Garnish each with whole pecan.

1 Cupcake: Calories 320; Total Fat 20g (Saturated Fat 8g, Trans Fat 1.5g); Cholesterol 50mg; Sodium 200mg; Total Carbohydrate 31g (Dietary Fiber 2g); Protein 3g **Exchanges:** 1 Starch, 1 Other Carbohydrate, 4 Fat **Carbohydrate Choices:** 2

Chocolate-Cherry Cupcakes

Prep Time: 40 Minutes • **Start to Finish:** 1 Hour 50 Minutes • Makes 24 cupcakes

1 box Betty Crocker SuperMoist devil's food cake mix

Water, vegetable oil and eggs called for on cake mix box

½ teaspoon almond extract, if desired

1 can (21 oz) cherry pie filling

2 containers (4 oz each) vanilla pudding

1 container (1 lb) Betty Crocker Rich & Creamy chocolate frosting

1 Heat oven to 350°F (325°F for dark or nonstick pans). Make and bake cake mix as directed on box for 24 cupcakes, adding almond extract to batter. Cool 10 minutes. Remove cupcakes from pans; place on cooling racks. Cool completely, about 30 minutes.

2 Just before serving, remove paper baking cups. Cut each cupcake crosswise into halves. On bottom half of each cupcake, spoon 1 tablespoon cherry pie filling; top with 2 teaspoons vanilla pudding. Replace top of cupcake.

3 Spoon frosting into small microwavable bowl. Microwave uncovered on High 30 seconds. Stir thoroughly until very soft and smooth, microwaving 5 to 15 seconds longer if necessary. Spoon 1 tablespoon frosting over top of cupcake. Top with 1 cherry from pie filling.

4 Repeat steps 2 and 3 with remaining cupcakes. Serve immediately.

1 Cupcake: Calories 230; Total Fat 9g (Saturated Fat 2g, Trans Fat 1g); Cholesterol 25mg; Sodium 220mg; Total Carbohydrate 35g (Dietary Fiber 0g); Protein 2g **Exchanges:** 1 Starch, 1½ Other Carbohydrate, 1½ Fat **Carbohydrate Choices:** 2

Tip Just the two of you? Wrap extra cupcakes tightly in plastic wrap, and freeze for up to 2 months.

Metric Conversion Guide

Volume

U.S. Units	Canadian Metric	Australian Metric
¼ teaspoon	1 mL	1 ml
½ teaspoon	2 mL	2 ml
1 teaspoon	5 mL	5 ml
1 tablespoon	15 mL	20 ml
¼ cup	50 mL	60 ml
⅓ cup	75 mL	80 ml
½ cup	125 mL	125 ml
⅔ cup	150 mL	170 ml
¾ cup	175 mL	190 ml
1 cup	250 mL	250 ml
1 quart	1 liter	1 liter
1½ quarts	1.5 liters	1.5 liters
2 quarts	2 liters	2 liters
2½ quarts	2.5 liters	2.5 liters
3 quarts	3 liters	3 liters
4 quarts	4 liters	4 liters

Weight

U.S. Units	Canadian Metric	Australian Metric
1 ounce	30 grams	30 grams
2 ounces	55 grams	60 grams
3 ounces	85 grams	90 grams
4 ounces (¼ pound)	115 grams	125 grams
8 ounces (½ pound)	225 grams	225 grams
16 ounces (1 pound)	455 grams	500 grams
1 pound	455 grams	0.5 kilogram

Note: The recipes in this cookbook have not been developed or tested using metric measures. When converting recipes to metric, some variations in quality may be noted.

Measurements

Inches	Centimeters
1	2.5
2	5.0
3	7.5
4	10.0
5	12.5
6	15.0
7	17.5
8	20.5
9	23.0
10	25.5
11	28.0
12	30.5
13	33.0

Temperatures

Fahrenheit	Celsius
32°	0°
212°	100°
250°	120°
275°	140°
300°	150°
325°	160°
350°	180°
375°	190°
400°	200°
425°	220°
450°	230°
475°	240°
500°	260°

Recipe Testing and Calculating Nutrition Information

Recipe Testing:

- Large eggs and 2% milk were used unless otherwise indicated.
- Fat-free, low-fat, low-sodium or lite products were not used unless indicated.
- No nonstick cookware and bakeware were used unless otherwise indicated. No dark-colored, black or insulated bakeware was used.
- When a pan is specified, a metal pan was used; a baking dish or pie plate means ovenproof glass was used.
- An electric hand mixer was used for mixing only when mixer speeds are specified.

Calculating Nutrition:

- The first ingredient was used wherever a choice is given, such as ⅓ cup sour cream or plain yogurt.
- The first amount was used wherever a range is given, such as 3- to 3½-pound whole chicken.
- The first serving number was used wherever a range is given, such as 4 to 6 servings.
- "If desired" ingredients were not included.
- Only the amount of a marinade or frying oil that is absorbed was included.

America's most trusted cookbook is better than ever!

- 1,100 all-new photos, including hundreds of step-by-step images
- More than 1,500 recipes, with hundreds of inspiring variations and creative "mini" recipes for easy cooking ideas
- Brand-new features
- Gorgeous new design

Get the best edition of the *Betty Crocker Cookbook* today!

www.ingramcontent.com/pod-product-compliance
Lightning Source LLC
Chambersburg PA
CBHW071418290426
44108CB00014B/1878